Practical Know-how
Teatime

SIMON &
SCHUSTER

LONDON • NEW YORK • SYDNEY • TORONTO

First published in Great Britain by
Simon & Schuster UK Ltd 2008
A CBS Company

Copyright © this compilation WI Enterprises Ltd, 2008
All rights reserved.
Illustrations copyright © Jane Norman 2008

ISBN 9 78184 737 2505

Simon and Schuster UK Ltd
Africa House
64–78 Kingsway
London WC2B 6AH

1 3 5 7 9 10 8 6 4 2

Design and illustrations by Jane Norman
Text by Jenny Kieldsen
Jacket design by Lizzie Gardiner
Printed and bound in China

Contents

Introduction

Tea (gathered from a type of camellia bush) has been a staple of China for centuries. One of the world's most refreshing and all-time great drinks, it has been praised for as long as it has been served. Tea was originally sold in Britain in pharmacies; it was very expensive and even kept under lock and key in a tea caddy! Today, tea is our national drink. It has lower caffeine levels than coffee, contains antioxidants, and counts towards the amount of fluid you should drink daily.

" Stands the Church clock at ten to three?
And is there honey still for tea?"

Rupert Brooke, 1887–1915

All about Tea

Time for tea

Between three and four o'clock in the afternoon
is considered to be the correct time
of day for tea.

Tea comes to Europe

The first tea brought to Europe was by a Portuguese missionary in 1560. It became very popular in Lisbon and, in the early 1600s, was shipped to the rest of Europe. These shipping costs were what made it so expensive – about £60 per pound weight.

Tea arrived in England in the mid 1650s and when Charles II married Catherine de Braganza (a Portuguese Princess) in 1662, a chest of tea was part of her dowry. Suddenly everyone was drinking tea, and it quickly replaced ale as the English national drink.

" *There are few hours in life more agreeable than the hour dedicated to the ceremony known as Afternoon Tea.* **"**

Henry James, 1843–1916

" *I always fear that creation will expire before tea time.* **"**

Sydney Smith, 1771–1845

The first teashop

In 1706 Thomas Twining served the first tea in London at Tom's Coffee House in The Strand. In 1717 this became the first teashop.

" *Come along inside...*
We'll see if tea and buns can make
the world a better place. **"**

Kenneth Grahame, 1859–1932,
The Wind in the Willows

Of course the choice is yours

The teas most commonly drunk at teatime are
Earl Grey, Darjeeling, Assam or, if you like
Chinese tea, Lapsang Souchong.

✳

If you like a good strong brew, leave it to 'mash'
or 'draw' in the pot for an extra 5 minutes.

Darjeeling

From India, this tea is often known as 'the
champagne' of teas. It has a smooth and rounded
muscatel flavour and a fantastic aroma.

✳

Assam

Also from India, Assam is full-bodied, fresh
tasting and subtle, with a 'malty', slightly
fragrant flavour and a bright colour

＊

Sri Lanka (Ceylon)

These delicate and fresh-tasting teas are grown
at very high altitudes.

＊

Earl Grey

Large leaves blended with bergamot for a fine,
delicate citrus flavour, Earl Grey can be drunk
with or without milk, or with a slice of lemon.

＊

13

Green tea

This is tea from China, Taiwan and Japan,
steamed and dried immediately after picking. It
is characterised by a delicate and refreshing
taste and is drunk without milk.

✳

Black tea

The process is the same as for green tea but,
after steaming, the tea is allowed to ferment
slightly in the open air. This enriches the flavour
and causes it to change colour, to black.

✳

Black tea grown by the Black Sea

This black tea is drunk all over Turkey. Served
in tall glasses without milk, it is very strong,
but very good and refreshing.

✳

Jasmine tea

This Chinese tea is blended with dried jasmine flowers. It is very delicate and refreshing, and is drunk without milk.

Lapsang Souchong

This is fermented black tea from China that has been lightly smoked. It has a fine and delicate flavour and can be drunk with or without milk.

White tea

From China, white tea is made with the downy
unopened buds of the tea plant. It has a light
aroma and misty flavour and is said to contain
more antioxidants than any other tea.
White tea is drunk without milk. Allow the
boiling water to cool a little before
pouring on to the tea.

※

Indian chai

This black tea, with added warming spices such
as cardamom, cloves and cinnamon, is very
refreshing. It is drunk with milk and, in India,
served already mixed with hot milk.

※

Herbal teas and infusions (tisanes)

Strictly speaking these are not teas. They do
not contain any tea leaves at all, and are
usually caffeine free. They are made from
natural ingredients such as fresh or dried edible
flowers and plants, such as chamomile,
peppermint and blackcurrant.

※

Redbush tea

Known also as Rooibos in Afrikaans, this is not
strictly a tea but a herbal remedy/tisane
gathered from a woody bush that only grows in
South Africa. It has a sweet and nutty taste
and is very high in antioxidants.

"*Tea is drunk to forget the din of the world.*"

Tien Yihing, c. 1570, Chinese poet

*

"*If you are cold, tea will warm you.*
If you are depressed, it will cheer you.
If you are excited, it will calm you."

William Gladstone, 1809–1898

The Moroccan way

In Morocco, green China tea is served, without milk, in small cups. Huge handfuls of fresh mint leaves and tea are brewed together (usually with sugar) to give a delicious and stimulating drink.

Sparkling mint tea
(a cooling cold drink)

Put 4 teaspoons of tea leaves into a teapot, and pour over 500 ml (1 pint) of boiling water. Stir then leave to infuse for 3–4 minutes. Strain into a large jug, adding 2–3 sprigs of fresh mint and 3 tablespoons of sugar. Stir well and leave to cool. Strain into tall glasses and top up with soda water and ice cubes. Garnish with some fresh mint and a slice of lemon.

" Come oh come ye tea-thirsty restless ones – the kettle boils, bubbles and sings, musically. "

Rabindranath Tagore, 1861–1941

To buy various Fairtrade teas:
www.fairtrade.org.uk and look under products/tea.

66 *'The dormouse is asleep again', said the Hatter, and he poured a little tea upon its nose.* 99

Lewis Carroll, 1832–1898,
Alice's Adventures in Wonderland

Making the Tea

Taste the difference

If the water in your area has a taste that you do
not like, or if it's very hard, try using bottled
water or a water purifier to make the tea.
It makes a huge difference.

A superior cup of tea

Until the mid 1700s, when porcelain (bone
china) was invented, tea was always
made in a silver pot.

In China, tea was always drunk in porcelain cups
with no handles, and these were imported for the
European aristocracy. The British wanted handles
on cups and this is how pottery companies (such
as Wedgwood and Royal Doulton) were able to
grow and become so wealthy.

There is no doubt that loose tea, made in a
bone china teapot and drunk from a bone china
cup is far superior to a bag in a mug.
Try it and see.

The perfect brew

Teabags are great when you are in a hurry, but loose tea in a teapot does taste quite different and nicer. Fill the kettle with freshly drawn water from the cold tap. Warm the teapot first with boiling water, empty this and then put in the tea (1 teaspoonful per person, more if you like strong tea). Boil the kettle again and pour the boiling water over the tea at the moment when it boils. Stir once, and leave to stand for 2–3 minutes. Cover with a tea cosy, if you wish.

How the teabag came to be

These were invented by accident in 1908. Thomas Sullivan, a New York tea merchant, started sending out tea samples in sealed silk bags. He discovered that his clients were not unwrapping the bags, but just pouring boiling water straight on to them.

"*A woman is like a teabag;
you never know how strong she is
until she gets into hot water.***"**

Eleanor Roosevelt, 1884–1962

Milk in first or last?

The choice, of course, is yours.

Milk in first: this was so that the scalding tea would not crack your best bone china cups, and because the milk becomes 'slightly cooked', giving the tea a more rounded flavour.

Milk in last: this came about because, in grand houses, the cream and sugar were handed around separately. Of course the thought of cream in tea is abhorrent to us now.

Making the Tea

" *The cup of tea on arrival at a country
house is a thing, which as a rule,
I particularly enjoy. I like the crackling logs,
the shadelights, the scent of buttered toast,
and the general atmosphere
of leisured cosiness.* **"**

P.G. Wodehouse, 1881–1975

Sugar cubes or lumps

A mixture of sugar crystals and sugar syrup, these were invented by Jakub Krystof Rad of Dacice (now in the Czech Republic), in 1841. There is even a large granite monument of a sugar cube in the centre of Dacice city.

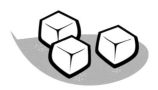

Tea with lemon

Earl Grey and other China teas are usually
served black with a slice of lemon, though they
are equally good with a little milk in first.

*

*Kissing is like drinking tea with a tea
strainer, you can never get enough.*

Anon.

> *"My hour for tea is half-past five, and my buttered toast waits for nobody."*

Wilkie Collins, 1824–1889, The Woman in White

Cakes and Biscuits

A tiered cake stand

This is great for biscuits and small cakes.
Teatime is a perfect time to use doilies, even if
they are a bit old-fashioned.

Shortbread biscuits

These are made in the proportions of 3, 2, 1:
75 g (3 oz) plain flour, 50 g (2 oz) butter, and
25g (1 oz) caster sugar, or 6, 4, 2. Put all the
ingredients into a bowl and rub in the butter
with your fingertips. Form the biscuit dough into
a ball and put in the fridge for 30 minutes. Roll
into a neat rectangle and place on a baking
sheet. Crimp the edges and prick all over with a
fork, then bake at Gas Mark 4/180°C/350°F
for about 25 minutes, until just golden.
Remove from the oven, cut immediately into
fingers, and cool on a wire rack.

To make 'Petticoat Tails'

Roll the dough into a neat circle, place on a
baking sheet, crimp the edges and prick all over
with a fork. When the shortbread is cooked,
cut the circle in half, then quarters
and then into 8 or 12 pieces.

Other shortbread ideas

To make really crisp and light shortbread, try
replacing just 1 oz flour with 1 oz rice flour.

Dip one half of each shortbread piece (when
cool) into melted chocolate. Leave to set
on silicone paper.

Bread and jam

Plain white bread and butter (cut very thin) is a staple of teatime. Serve some good jams to spread over: damson, raspberry, Little Scarlet (strawberry) or any homemade jam.

66 *The King asked*
The Queen, and
The Queen asked
The Dairymaid:
'Could we have some butter for
The Royal slice of bread?'
The Queen asked
The Dairymaid
The Dairymaid
Said, 'Certainly,
I'll go and tell
The cow
Now
Before she goes to bed'. 99

A.A Milne, 1882 1956

Welsh cakes

(old recipe so no metric)

Into a large bowl put 8 oz plain flour, 1 level teaspoon baking powder and 1 teaspoon mixed spice then rub in 4 oz butter (you could use half lard). Add 3 oz caster sugar, 3 oz currants, 1 egg and a little milk to bind, to make a firm dough. Roll out the dough on a floured surface to ¼ in thick and cut into small circles using a cutter. Heat a non-stick frying pan and very lightly grease the surface with butter. Cook the Welsh cakes for about 3 minutes each side until they are golden brown. Cool on a wire rack and dust with caster sugar to serve.

Scones

Into a large bowl put 225 g (8 oz) plain flour
and 1 heaped teaspoon of baking powder; rub
in 25 g (1 oz) butter. Add 150 ml (¼ pint) milk.
Bring together to make a soft but not sticky
dough. Roll out very lightly on a floured surface
to about 2.5 cm (1 inch) thick. Cut into circles,
using a small plain round cutter, and place on a
floured baking sheet. Cook the scones for
12–15 minutes at Gas Mark 7/220°C/425°F
until well risen and golden.

✺

Sour milk (just 'turning') is very good for
making scones; they will be lighter
and better risen.

66 *It snowed last year: I made a snowman and my brother knocked it down and I knocked my brother down and then we had tea.* **99**

Dylan Thomas, 1914–1953

Cream tea

Serve the scones just warm, with clotted cream and jam. Whether you put the jam or cream on first is entirely your choice, but in Devon and Cornwall there is a debate about which is best. The Cornish go for jam first and the Devonians go for cream first.

Feeding a fruitcake

Fruitcake is traditional at teatime; you could try 'feeding' it beforehand. Prick the bottom of the cake with a fork and pour over a couple of tablespoons of either brandy or whisky, repeat 2–3 times, keeping the cake wrapped in foil.

Icing sugar pattern for a Victoria sandwich

Another good choice for tea is a Victoria sponge
filled with jam, or jam and cream. Lay a lace or
paper doily over the cake and shake over some
sieved icing sugar; this will leave a very pretty
pattern on the surface of the cake.

Lemon drizzle cake

Into a food processor put 125 g (4 oz) butter, 175 g (6 oz) sugar, 175 g (6 oz) self-raising flour, 2 eggs, 4 tablespoons of milk, and the finely grated rind of 1 lemon. Whiz until everything is well mixed. Pour into a greased 21 cm (8 inch) square cake tin and bake for about 50 minutes at Gas Mark 4/180°C/350°F until the cake is firm and springy to the touch.

In a small saucepan, over a low heat, mix together the juice of 1 lemon with 3 tablespoons of icing sugar. Prick the hot surface of the cake with a fork, and spoon the syrup over. Leave the cake in the tin until cold and either serve whole or cut into nine squares.

For a very special treat

Try dipping some strawberries in melted dark or
white chocolate; leave the stalk on, as this
makes dipping easier. Cool on silicon paper,
and serve in small (*petits fours*) paper
cases, if you can find them.

" *Tea – the cup that cheers,
but not inebriates.* "

William Cowper, 1731–1800

✳

" *The most popular non-alcoholic drink
is Tea, now considered almost
a necessary of life.* "

Mrs Beeton, 1836–1865

66 '*Take some more tea*', *the March Hare*
said to Alice, very earnestly. 'I've had
nothing yet' Alice replied in an offended
tone, 'so I can't take more'. 99

Lewis Carroll, 1832–1898,
Alice's Adventures in Wonderland

Savouries and High Tea

Tea or supper?

High tea is a direct survival of the 17th century
habit of having dinner at 5pm; later in the
evening another small meal was served
known as 'rear supper'.

Savoury before sweet

It is traditional to serve the savoury food first at teatime.

'Teatime' is born

The 7th Duchess of Bedford, was thought to be the first aristocrat to ask her butler to serve her tea and a few savoury and sweet tit-bits in the afternoon, because she was hungry between lunch and dinner. This was in the 1840s in The Blue Room at Woburn Abbey, and thus Teatime was born.

" *Tea to the English is really
a picnic indoors.* **"**

Alice Walker, b. 1944

" *T'is pity wine be so deleterious, for tea
and coffee leave us much more serious.* **"**

Lord Byron, 1788–1824

Northern tea

In the north of England, at weekends, tea is often a more elaborate affair than just a cuppa and a biscuit. Cold meats and salad, followed by cakes and fruit salad are served at teatime. Supper might be a sandwich and hot drink before bedtime.

Teatime sandwiches

Remove the crusts from the sandwiches then
cut into either triangles or fingers and arrange
on a plate. You could add some cucumber
twists, celery sticks or radishes to
the plate if you wish.

Cucumber sandwiches

These are a staple of teatime. Peel the
cucumber and slice as thinly as possible.
Spread white or brown bread with butter, add
the cucumber slices and sprinkle on a little salt
and freshly ground black pepper.

Unusual sandwich filling

Grate some cheese (Cheddar is good) and mix
with some finely chopped celery and a little
mayonnaise to bind. There's no need
to butter the bread.

Watercress sandwiches

Try to buy watercress in bunches, not sealed in
a plastic bag. Wash well, remove the top third
from the watercress (the rest will make soup)
and chop roughly. Use to fill the sandwiches –
brown bread is best.

The Gentlemen's Relish

Also known as *Patum Peperium*, this is a delicious spiced anchovy relish, which also contains butter, herbs and spices. It was created in 1828 by Englishman, John Osborn, and is still popular today. It should be spread sparingly on thin hot toast then cut into fingers or triangles.

" *When the tea is brought at five o'clock,*
And all the neat curtains are drawn with care,
The little black cat with bright green eyes
Is suddenly purring there. **"**

Harold Munro, 1879–1932, 'Milk for the Cat'

Cheese straws

Rub 50 g (2 oz) butter into 125 g (4½ oz) plain flour; add 50 g (2 oz) strong grated cheese and a good pinch of chilli powder. Bring together with about 2 tablespoons of cold water then rest in the fridge for 30 minutes. Roll out into a long rectangle and with a large sharp knife cut into thin strips. Carefully place on a baking sheet and bake at Gas Mark 6/200°C/400°F for about 15 minutes until crisp and golden. Sprinkle with a little salt and serve piled up on a plate.

High Tea

This is very popular in Scotland. It is usually taken at 6pm and is a much more substantial affair than English tea. Bread, butter and jam and then cakes would be served after the main course of a cooked dish, such as eggs or cheese on toast, or fish.

'Ham and haddie'

This dish comes from the Moray Firth in Scotland. Poached smoked haddock (never the dyed bright yellow kind) is placed on top of a slice of smoked ham, seasoned with freshly ground pepper and a good splash of cream. It is then grilled until hot and golden brown.

Smoked poached haddock

This smoked haddock dish is served with a poached egg on top of the fish and bread and butter on the side.

Ways to poach an egg

Always try to use a fresh, free-range egg. You can either use an egg poacher, which steams the eggs over hot water in little non-stick 'cups' (the eggs are always very neat and easy to do) or try the original method below.

＊

Half-fill a small saucepan with water, bring to the boil and add about 2–3 drops of vinegar (helps to set the egg); any more would make it taste vinegary. Turn the heat down as low as possible and crack the egg into a teacup. Swirl the water around and slide the egg in (the revolving water will help the egg to keep a good shape). Cook for about 3–4 minutes until set then remove the egg with a slotted spoon and drain on kitchen paper.

You could use a frying pan filled with water but,
until you become proficient at poaching, only do
one egg at a time. They will keep warm in
a low oven (on kitchen paper).

Cheese on toast

This is a good High Tea staple. Grill the toast on one side first then spread the other side with a little butter. Cover with slices of a good flavoured Cheddar, taking it right to the edge of the toast so that the crusts don't burn, then grill until golden.

Extras for cheese on toast

Lea & Perrins Worcestershire Sauce is really good shaken over the cheese before grilling.

✻

Mix a little finely sliced onion or shallot with the cheese.

✻

Thinly slice a tomato on top of the cheese halfway though grilling.

※

Place a poached egg on top of the grilled cheese.

※

Spread Gentlemen's Relish (*Patum Peperium*)
on the toast before the cheese, or shake a
little anchovy essence on the cheese.

※

Try half Cheddar and half Stilton.

※

Spread a little mustard on the toast before
adding the cheese; either French for a mild
flavour or English if you like it hot.

※

Mix grated cheese with a little milk to make the
cheese more 'bubbly'.

※

Serve with some fruit chutney.

Potato cakes

Into a bowl put 225 g (8 oz) self-raising flour,
1 teaspoon salt, and then rub in 100 g (3½ oz)
butter. Add 175 g (6 oz) warm mashed potato
and a little milk and mix into a soft dough. Roll
out to 2 cm (¾ inch) thick and cut into rounds.
Bake the cakes on a floured baking sheet at Gas
Mark 6/200°C/400°F for about 20 minutes.
Cool, then split in half and spread with
butter to serve.

Caraway seeds are very good sprinkled onto
the potato cakes just before they are cooked –
brush with a little milk first.

" *My tea is nearly ready and the*
sun has left the sky;
It's time to take the window to see
Leerie going by;
For every night at teatime and before you
take your seat,
With lantern and with ladder he comes
posting up the street. **"**

Robert Louis Stevenson, 1850–1894,
'The Lamplighter'

Fruit tea loaf

Soaking the fruit in tea gives this cake extra flavour. The cake will improve if kept for a few days before cutting.

150 g (5 oz) mixed fruit

✴

1 good strong teabag (your choice)

✴

100 g (3½ oz) soft margarine

✴

100 g (3½ oz) caster sugar

✴

1 level teaspoon mixed spice

✴

1 egg

✴

200 g (7 oz) self-raising flour

Put the teabag and mixed fruit into a bowl and pour over boiling water to cover, give a good stir, and leave until the tea is cold.
Drain in a colander.

Put the flour into a deep bowl, add the margarine and rub in with your fingertips until the mixture resembles breadcrumbs.

Add all the other ingredients and beat well with a wooden spoon. The mixture should just drop from the end of the spoon. If it is a little stiff, add a couple of tablespoons of milk.

Turn into a greased and lined (or use a cake liner) loaf tin 12 cm x 24 cm x 6 cm deep (2 lb). Bake at Gas Mark 4/180°C/350°F for 45–50 minutes until the cake is risen, golden and firm to the touch. Leave to cool in the tin.

" *Tea tempers the spirit and harmonises the mind; dispels lassitude and relieves fatigue, awakens thought and prevents drowsiness.* **"**

Lu Yu, the 'Sage of Tea', 733–804

Laying the Table

To protect a good polished table

Put a blanket, or similar, under the cloth to
protect the surface of the table. You could also
use a heat-resistant mat for the teapot
to stand on.

A white linen cloth

The right setting for teatime is either a plain white cloth or one with some pretty embroidery on it; matching linen napkins would be perfect too, although good paper napkins work just as well.

If you're worried about stains on your best white linen tablecloth, put a smaller white or coloured cotton or paper cloth over the centre part of the table.

To remove tea stains from a linen cloth

Use either Borax (a water softener) or washing soda crystals. Mix 1 tablespoonful with a teacup of warm water. Lay the stained area of the cloth over a bowl and pour the water and crystals over it. Leave to stand for 30 minutes then wash in the normal way.

❋

For Borax and other 'green' household cleaning items, check the Internet.

"*The privileges of the side-table included the small prerogatives of sitting next to the toast, and taking two cups of tea to other people's one.***"**

Charles Dickens, 1812–1870

To starch a linen cloth

Use some old-fashioned starch and follow the manufacturer's instructions. Don't make the cloth too stiff; if you do, it will not 'sit' properly on the tea table.

To iron an embroidered cloth and napkins

It is much easier to iron a cloth when it is slightly damp; use the iron on the highest heat (for linen), making sure that it's scrupulously clean. To make the embroidery stand out, iron on the reverse of the pattern last.

❝ To test tea, drop a pinch in the fire: the bluer the blaze the better the tea. ❞

Mrs Beeton, 1836–1865

❝ Remember the tea kettle – it is always up to its neck in hot water, yet still sings. ❞

Anon.

Removing tea stains from teacups, here are two good ideas:

Using a kitchen towel, rub the stained areas with a little salt or bicarbonate of soda. The abrasive action will remove the stains.

Soak the cups for an hour or overnight in a solution of washing soda (1 cup of soda to 600 ml/1 pint water). Wash and rinse thoroughly afterwards.

Sugar bowl

Use a small bowl for the sugar or sugar lumps/cubes. Sugar tongs are traditionally used with sugar lumps, although nowadays few people have them and they are regarded as pretentious.

66 *Strange how a teapot can represent at the same time the comforts of solitude and the pleasures of company.* **99**

Anon.

Bone china tea service

If you have one, with matching tea plates, use
it for a special occasion. Small knives and
teaspoons are the only cutlery needed. Jam is
nice decanted into a pretty jam pot
with a lid and a jam spoon.

“ *Never trust a man who,*
when left alone in a room with a tea cosy,
doesn't try it on! **”**

Billy Connolly, b. 1942, Scottish comedian

Serving savoury foods

These should be served on 'dish papers'
(available in some stores). They are plain paper
covers, usually oval. Make a pleat in the middle
if you're using a round plate.

" '*Pooh*', *he said,* '*Christopher Robin is giving a party.*' '*Oh!*' *said Pooh,* '*Will there be those little cake things with pink sugar icing?*'**"**

A.A Milne, 1882–1956

Tea Parties

A very social occasion

In many cultures tea is a focal point for social gatherings, particularly in Arab countries and in Japan. In late Victorian times tea dances at Grand Hotels, and specially laid-out tea gardens, changed the social life of Britain.

A child's birthday tea

Always remember that children do not eat as much food as you would expect, so keep it simple. Let your children choose bright paper cloths, napkins and paper cups.

✳

Remove the crusts from sandwiches then cut them into shapes with cookie cutters.

✳

Serve tiny cooked sausages. You can use cocktail sticks for older children, but for younger ones hands are fine!

Tea Parties

✳

Cut carrots and cucumber into small sticks, and dip into cream cheese softened with a little milk and tomato ketchup.

✳

Thread grapes on sticks to dip into Greek yogurt, sweetened with a little sugar and vanilla essence.

✳

Serve fruit jellies, set in individual paper bowls.

✳

Make a sponge mix and put it into small bun cases. When the little cakes are cooked let the children ice and decorate them.

" *Another novelty is the tea-party,*
an extraordinary meal in that, being offered
to persons that have already dined well,
it supposes neither appetite nor thirst,
and has no object but distraction,
no basis but delicate enjoyment. **"**

Anthelme Brillat-Savarin, 1755–1826

Cornflake or rice crispies

Get your child or children to help. Melt 175 g (6 oz) chocolate and 1 tablespoon of golden syrup in a bowl in the microwave or over hot water. Add enough cornflakes or rice crispies to soak up the chocolate mixture. Put the crispies into small paper cases and leave to set.

❝ *The iron kettle sings on the stove.*
She cuts some bread and says to the child,
'It's time for tea now'. **❞**

Elizabeth Bishop, 1911–1979

Dolls' and teddies' tea party

For younger ones, ask every child to bring their
favourite teddy or doll to sit at the
table with them.

Young children love tea sets: they can lay out
plastic plates and cups for their toys and either
pretend to feed them mini sandwiches and
cakes or eat the food themselves! They love
to pour the 'tea' into the cups from
a little teapot.

" *I'm a little teapot short and stout.*

Here's my handle, here's my spout.

When I get all steamed up, hear me shout.

Just tip me over and pour me out. **"**

American rhyme

Try a tea-tasting party

Why not have a tea party to sample some new and different types of tea (rather like a wine tasting)? You would need a few extra teapots and cups, or you could use small (demitasse) coffee cups, so that your guests could sample a range of different teas. Make sure you have still or sparkling water to clean the palate between each tasting. You could even ask your guests to mark the teas out of 10 and with what they would accompany each tea.

Some ideas:
Lapsang Souchong, Darjeeling, Green tea,
Redbush, cold mint tea.

❝ *A proper tea is much nicer than A Very Nearly Tea, which is one you forget about afterwards.* **❞**

A.A Milne, 1882–1956

The Boston Tea Party, 1773

All the tea that was shipped to the US was from Britain. When the British Government decided to put huge taxes on tea, the Boston wives refused to buy it. Eventually, their husbands (the local merchants) dressed as Native Americans and raided the tea clippers in the harbour. They tipped at least 340 chests of tea into the ocean. This is thought to have been a trigger for the American War of Independence.

Even if you're having a children's tea party, the adults can still enjoy themselves!

Coffee and walnut cake
(maybe with a glass of sherry!)

Cream together 175 g (6 oz) soft margarine and 175 g (6 oz) caster sugar, either by hand or in a food processor, until soft and fluffy. Gradually add 3 beaten eggs, and then stir in 175 g (6 oz) self-raising flour and 90 g (3 oz) finely chopped walnuts. The mixture should be a soft, dropping consistency.

Put into two greased and lined 6-inch cake tins and bake at Gas Mark 6/200°C/400°F for 20 minutes until the cakes are golden and well risen. Cool on a wire rack.

Coffee icing

Cream together 90 g (3 oz) butter with 90 g
(3 oz) icing sugar and then beat in 3 teaspoons
of good instant coffee dissolved in 1 tablespoon
of boiling water. Use this to sandwich the
cakes together, and to smooth over the top.
Decorate with 8 whole walnut halves.

❋

The cake can be made in advance and frozen,
then iced on the day.

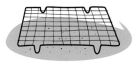

" *She was of the stuff of which great men's mothers are made. She was indispensable to high generation, hated at tea parties, feared in shops, and loved at crises.* **"**

Thomas Hardy, 1840–1928

Take-home cake

If there's some cake left over, it's a nice idea
to give children or adults a piece to take home.
Just wrap a slice in foil, greaseproof paper
or a napkin for each guest.

"*Thank God for tea!*

What would the world do without tea!

How did it exist?

*I am glad I was not born before tea.***"**

Sydney Smith, 1771–1845